Unveiling The Devices Of The Enemy

Biblical Examples and Insights

Dr. Robert Osobase

UNVEILING THE DEVICES OF THE ENEMY
Biblical Examples and Insights

Copyright ©2024 By Dr. Robert Osobase

Paperback ISBN: 978-1-957809-88-5

All rights reserved. No part of this publication may be reproduced, distributed, or transmitted in any form or by any means, including photocopying, recording, or other electronic or mechanical methods without the prior written permission of the author except in the case of brief quotations embodied in reviews and certain other non-commercial uses permitted by copyright law.

Published by Cornerstone Publishing

A Division of Cornerstone Creativity Group LLC
Info@thecornerstonepublishers.com
www.thecornerstonepublishers.com

Author's Contact

To book the author to speak at your next event or to order bulk copies of this book, please, use the information below:

rovic72@gmail.com

Printed in the United States of America.

DEDICATION

To the Glory of God Almighty, and to my Savior, Jesus Christ, whose unwavering love and boundless grace have guided me through the valleys and peaks of life. May this book bring glory to your name and inspire hearts to seek your eternal light.

CONTENTS

DEDICATION ii
INTRODUCTION vi

1. Understandin Spiritual Warfare 1
2. The Deception Of The Serpent: Lessons From Adam And Eve 11
3. The Temptation Of David - Overcoming Personal Weakness 15
4. Jezebel's Influence: Confronting Manipulative Spirits. 21
5. Testing Job's Faith Amid Trials 27
6. The Doubts Of Thomas: Building Stronger Belief Systems 33
7. The Pride Of Nebuchadnezzar: Humility And God's Sovereignty 37
8. The Betrayal Of Judas: Recognizing The Dangers Of Betrayal 41
9. The Fear Of Elijah: Overcoming Fear And Anxiety... 45
10. The Pharisees' Hypocrisy: Living With Authenticity... 51

11. Peter's Denial: Embracing Forgiveness And Restoration 59
12. The Rebellion Of Korah: Submission To God-Ordained Authority 63
13. The Manipulation Of Delilah: Guarding Against Emotional Manipulation 67
14. The Frustration Of Jonah: Surrendering To God's Will 73
15. The Battles Of Paul: Perseverance And Endurance In Ministry 77

CONCLUSION 81

Introduction

Unveiling the Devices of the Enemy using biblical examples and insights delves into the intricate nature of spiritual warfare by examining significant events and characters from the Bible. This enlightening book seeks to equip believers with a deeper understanding of the strategies employed by the enemy and provides valuable insights on how to overcome them.

In today's world, the spiritual realm often goes unnoticed or underestimated. However, by exploring the timeless wisdom found within the pages of Scripture, we can uncover the subtle devices used by the enemy to derail our faith, hinder our progress, and sow seeds of doubt. Through these biblical examples, we gain practical knowledge on how to discern and counteract the enemy's tactics.

Each chapter of this book focuses on a specific story or character, drawing out key lessons and principles that apply to our lives today. From the deceptive schemes of the serpent in the Garden of Eden to the battles faced by the apostle Paul, we embark on a journey of discovery and growth. By examining these accounts, we gain valuable insights into recognizing and overcoming spiritual warfare in our own lives.

Unveiling the Devices of the Enemy is not just a theoretical exploration; it offers practical guidance for believers seeking to live victoriously in their spiritual journey. This book serves as a comprehensive resource for individuals, small groups, and church communities, equipping them with the tools necessary to identify and resist the devices of the enemy.

Prepare to be enlightened, encouraged, and empowered as you delve into the pages of Unveiling the Devices of the Enemy: Biblical Examples and Insights. May this book inspire you to stand firm in your faith, knowing that greater is He who is in you than he who is in the world.

CHAPTER 1
Understanding Spiritual Warfare

Spiritual warfare is a concept that is often associated with religious or spiritual belief systems. It refers to the idea that there is a battle or conflict taking place in the spiritual realm between good and evil forces. This battle is believed to have a direct influence on the physical world and the lives of individuals.

In many religious traditions, spiritual warfare is seen as a struggle between God or a higher power and opposing forces such as Satan, demons, or other malevolent beings. The purpose of spiritual warfare is typically to overcome and defeat these negative forces to bring about spiritual growth, personal transformation, and the establishment of divine will on Earth. The foundation of spiritual warfare in Christianity is rooted in biblical teachings. Christians believe that Satan, a fallen angel who rebelled against God, is the adversary and enemy of both God and humanity. Satan is depicted as a deceiver and tempter, seeking to lead people away from God and into spiritual bondage.

According to Christian belief, spiritual warfare involves resisting the influence and attacks of Satan and his demonic forces through prayer, faith, and the power of the Holy Spirit. Christians are encouraged to put on the armor of God, as described in Ephesians 6:10-18, which includes the belt of truth, the breastplate of righteousness, the shield of faith, the helmet of salvation, the sword of the Spirit (which is the word of God), and the feet fitted with the readiness of the gospel of peace. These symbolic pieces of armor represent spiritual attributes and disciplines that help believers stand firm against spiritual opposition.

KEY ELEMENTS TO UNDERSTANDING SPIRITUAL WARFARE

1. Recognizing the Existence of the Spiritual Realm:

Spiritual warfare presupposes the existence of a realm beyond the physical world that is populated by spiritual beings, both good and evil. This realm is believed to influence and interact with the physical world. In Christianity, the existence of the spiritual realm is a fundamental belief.

Christians derive this belief from the teachings of the Bible, personal experiences, encounters with God, and the life and teachings of Jesus Christ. The spiritual realm is considered real and significant, with implications for one's relationship with God and the understanding of the nature of reality. Additionally, Jesus Christ, who is central to the Christian faith, acknowledged the reality of the spiritual realm. He frequently spoke about God, heaven, and hell, emphasizing the eternal nature of the soul and the importance of spiritual matters. Jesus' own resurrection from the dead further confirms the existence of the spiritual realm.

2. Identifying the Opposition:

Spiritual warfare involves identifying the opposing forces, which are often seen as evil or demonic entities. These forces may be understood as working against the well-being and spiritual progress of individuals or communities. For Christians, opposition can be interpreted in different ways. It can refer to various groups or ideologies that oppose or differ from mainstream Christian beliefs, teachings, or practices. Some oppositions within Christianity include:

- Atheists who reject the existence of God worshipped by Christians. They may challenge Christian beliefs and engage in debates and discussions to promote their worldview.

- Agnostics believe that the existence of God or ultimate truth is unknown or unknowable. They may not outright oppose Christianity but maintain skepticism and uncertainty regarding religious claims.

- Secularists advocate for the separation of religious institutions and beliefs from the public sphere. They argue for a society where religious influence is minimized or removed from government, education, and policymaking.

- Christianity faces opposition from other religious traditions, such as Judaism, Islam, Hinduism, Buddhism, and others. These religions have distinct belief systems and practices that often differ from Christian teachings.

- There are various religious movements or cults that deviate significantly from traditional Christian beliefs and practices. Examples include Jehovah's Witnesses, Mormons (Latter-day Saints), and Christian Science.

- Liberal Christians interpret and apply Christian teachings in a more progressive and inclusive manner. They may question or reject certain traditional doctrines or emphasize social justice issues that can be at odds with more conservative or orthodox Christian views.

- Some ideologies, such as communism, Marxism, or certain forms of radical feminism, have historically opposed or sought to suppress Christianity due to ideological conflicts or differing views on social, political, or economic matters.

The degree of opposition can vary within each group or individual, and not all members will hold the same views or exhibit hostility towards Christianity. Additionally, within Christianity itself, there can be internal disagreements and opposition between different denominations, sects, or theological perspectives.

3. Engaging in Battle:

Spiritual warfare involves actively engaging in battle against negative forces. This engagement can take various forms, such as prayer, fasting, meditation, worship, or performing specific rituals or ceremonies. The purpose is to combat the influence of evil and bring about positive change. As a Christian, engaging in spiritual battle is an important aspect of one's faith. The Bible provides numerous examples of individuals who faced spiritual battles and offers guidance on how to navigate and overcome them. Biblical examples demonstrate that engaging in spiritual battles requires relying on God's strength, prayer, faith, and adherence to God's Word. Christians can draw inspiration and guidance from these stories as they navigate their own spiritual battles.

In the Gospel accounts, Jesus faced various spiritual battles, including His temptation in the wilderness by Satan (Matthew 4:1-11). Jesus relied on Scripture and the power of God's Word to resist temptation and emerge victorious. King David encountered spiritual battles throughout his life, both physically and spiritually. One notable example is his encounter with Goliath, a Philistine giant who taunted the armies of Israel. David, relying on his faith in God, defeated Goliath with a single stone (1 Samuel 17). The prophet Elijah contended with the prophets of Baal on Mount Carmel (1 Kings 18). He challenged the false prophets to a test to determine whose God was the true God. Through prayer and faith, Elijah witnessed God's power and emerged victorious. Paul experienced numerous spiritual battles during his ministry. In Ephesians 6:10-18, he encourages believers to put on the armor of God to stand firm against the schemes of the devil. He emphasizes the importance of truth, righteousness, faith, salvation, and the Word of God in overcoming spiritual battles. Job's story illustrates a spiritual battle on a personal level. Job faced immense suffering and loss, but he remained faithful to God despite the accusations and temptations of Satan. In the end, Job's faithfulness was rewarded, and he experienced restoration (Job 1-42).

4. Equipping Oneself:

To effectively engage in spiritual warfare, individuals often seek to equip themselves with spiritual tools and resources.

Equipping oneself with Bible scriptures is a powerful way to engage in spiritual warfare. Here are some key verses that can help you in your battle:

Ephesians 6:10-11 - "Finally, be strong in the Lord and in his mighty power. Put on the full armor of God so that you can take your stand against the devil's schemes." Explanation: This passage emphasizes the need to rely on God's strength and put on the spiritual armor to resist the schemes of the enemy.

2 Corinthians 10:3-5 - "For though we live in the world, we do not wage war as the world does. The weapons we fight with are not the weapons of the world. On the contrary, they have divine power to demolish strongholds. We demolish arguments and every pretension that sets itself up against the knowledge of God, and we take captive every thought to make it obedient to Christ." Explanation: This verse highlights the spiritual nature of the battle and encourages believers to rely on God's power to tear down strongholds and bring every thought into obedience to Christ.

James 4:7 - "Submit yourselves, then, to God. Resist the devil, and he will flee from you." Explanation: This verse teaches the importance of submitting to God and actively resisting the devil. When we stand firm against the enemy, he will eventually flee.

1 Peter 5:8-9 - "Be alert and of sober mind. Your enemy the devil prowls around like a roaring lion looking for someone to devour. Resist him, standing firm in the faith, because you know that the family of believers throughout the world is undergoing the same kind of sufferings." Explanation: This passage reminds us to be watchful and vigilant, recognizing that the devil seeks to devour and destroy. By standing firm in our faith, we can resist him.

Romans 8:37-39 - "No, in all these things we are more than conquerors through him who loved us. For I am convinced that neither death nor life, neither angels nor demons, neither the present nor the future, nor any powers, neither height nor depth, nor anything else in all creation, will be able to separate us from the love of God that is in Christ Jesus our Lord." Explanation: This verse affirms our victory through Christ and assures us that nothing can separate us from God's love. It reinforces our confidence in battling spiritual forces.

Remember that these scriptures are not mere words, but the living and active Word of God. Regularly meditate on them, internalize their truth, and apply them in your spiritual warfare.

UNDERSTANDING THE NATURE OF THE BATTLE

Spiritual warfare is often seen as a continuous struggle that takes place on multiple levels, including the personal, interpersonal, and societal levels. It is believed that the outcome of this battle has far-reaching implications for both the individual and the world at large. The Bible teaches that Christians are engaged in a spiritual battle against spiritual forces of darkness. Ephesians 6:12 states, "For our struggle is not against flesh and blood, but against the rulers, against the authorities, against the powers of this dark world and against the spiritual forces of evil in the heavenly realms." This battle is not fought with physical weapons but with spiritual armor, as mentioned in the subsequent verses of Ephesians 6. The nature of the spiritual battle can be understood in several ways including temptation and sin, false teachings and deception, prayer and spiritual warfare, growth, and transformation, and engaging in good works.

DISCERNING GOOD AND EVIL

A crucial aspect of spiritual warfare is the ability to discern between good and evil. This involves developing spiritual discernment and cultivating a deep connection with one's faith or spiritual beliefs. The Bible encourages Christians to develop discernment to navigate this spiritual warfare effectively. In the New Testament, the apostle Paul writes in Ephesians 6:12, "For our struggle is not against flesh and blood, but against the rulers, against the authorities, against the powers of this dark world and against the spiritual forces of evil in the heavenly realms." This verse highlights the spiritual nature of the battle and emphasizes the need for discernment. Discernment involves being able to evaluate thoughts, actions, and situations considering biblical truth. It requires a deep understanding of God's Word, the Bible, which serves as the ultimate standard of truth for Christians. Through prayer, seeking wisdom from

God, and studying Scripture, believers can develop the ability to discern what is good and pleasing to God and what is evil and contrary to His will.

Prayer is considered a vital weapon in spiritual warfare, as it is seen to communicate with God and seek His guidance, protection, and strength. Christians are encouraged to pray for themselves, others, and even their enemies, asking God to intervene and overcome the forces of darkness. Additionally, spiritual warfare also involves personal spiritual growth and sanctification. Christians are encouraged to cultivate a deep relationship with God, study the Scriptures, and live according to biblical principles. This includes resisting temptations, renewing the mind, and developing a discerning spirit to recognize and combat spiritual attacks. It is important to note that while spiritual warfare is acknowledged in Christianity, it is not a call to fear or obsession with demonic activity. The focus is ultimately on God's power, victory, and the hope found in Jesus Christ. Christians are encouraged to trust in God's sovereignty and rely on His strength to overcome spiritual battles, knowing that through Christ, they have the ultimate victory over evil.

CHAPTER 2
The Deception Of The Serpent: Lessons From Adam And Eve

The biblical story of Adam and Eve in the Garden of Eden is one of the most well-known narratives in human history. It serves as a cautionary tale, highlighting the consequences of deception and disobedience. Through the cunning manipulation of the serpent, Adam and Eve fell into temptation and committed the original sin, forever altering the course of humanity. In Genesis 3, the serpent, often identified as Satan or the devil, approaches Eve and engages her in conversation. The serpent cunningly questions Eve about the fruit of the tree in the middle of the garden, which God had forbidden them to eat from. The serpent says to Eve, "Did God actually say, 'You shall not eat of any tree in the garden'?" (Genesis 3:1, ESV). This story carries profound lessons that are applicable to our lives even today.

Lesson 1: The Nature of Deception The serpent in the Garden of Eden exemplifies the art of deception. It cunningly approached Eve and questioned God's commandment, planting doubt in her mind. The serpent twisted the truth, convincing Eve that by eating the forbidden fruit, she would attain knowledge and become like God. This teaches us that deception often disguises itself as something desirable, appealing to our desires and aspirations. It reminds us to be vigilant and discerning, not easily swayed by enticing promises that may lead us astray.

Lesson 2: The Consequences of Disobedience Adam and Eve's disobedience resulted in severe consequences for both and future generations. They were banished from the Garden of Eden, symbolizing the loss of their close relationship with God and the introduction of pain, suffering, and mortality into the world. This teaches us the gravity of our actions and the ripple effects they can have. Disobedience to moral principles and divine commandments can lead to detrimental consequences, affecting not only our own lives but also those around us.

Lesson 3: The Importance of Personal Responsibility After realizing their mistake, Adam and Eve attempted to shift the blame onto others. Adam blamed Eve, and Eve blamed the serpent. However, they both ultimately faced the consequences of their actions. This teaches us the significance of personal responsibility and accountability. We must acknowledge our choices and their consequences, accepting the role we play in shaping our lives. Blaming others only hinders personal growth and prevents us from learning from our mistakes.

Lesson 4: The Power of Forgiveness and Redemption Despite the gravity of Adam and Eve's sin, the story offers a glimmer of hope through the promise of redemption. God, in His mercy, provides them with garments and promises a Savior who will ultimately reconcile humanity with Him. This demonstrates the power of forgiveness and the opportunity for personal redemption. No matter how far we may have strayed, there is always a chance to seek forgiveness, learn from our mistakes, and strive for spiritual growth.

The story of Adam and Eve serves as a timeless reminder of the consequences of deception and disobedience. It emphasizes the importance of being discerning, taking personal responsibility for our actions, and seeking forgiveness when we falter. By reflecting on these lessons, we can navigate life's challenges with wisdom and integrity, striving for a deeper understanding of ourselves and our relationship with the divine. The story serves as an account of the origin of human sin and the separation between humanity and God. It illustrates the dangers of succumbing to temptation and highlights the consequences of disobedience. The narrative is often interpreted as a cautionary tale about the need to trust and obey God's commands rather than being deceived by worldly temptations.

CHAPTER 3

The Temptation Of David - Overcoming Personal Weakness

In the journey of life, each individual faces personal weaknesses that can often lead to difficult and challenging situations. These weaknesses can manifest in various forms, testing one's character and resolve. The story of David, the renowned king of ancient Israel, provides us with valuable insights into the temptations and personal weaknesses that can befall even the most revered figures.

One significant event that is often associated with David's temptation is his affair with Bathsheba, as described in 2

Samuel chapter 11. Despite knowing that she was married, David gave in to his temptation and sent messengers to bring Bathsheba to him. David and Bathsheba engaged in an adulterous relationship, and as a result, Bathsheba became pregnant. David, trying to cover up his wrongdoing, summoned Uriah back from the battlefield in the hope that he would sleep with his wife and assume the child was his. However, Uriah's loyalty to his fellow soldiers and commitment to the war effort prevented him from going home to Bathsheba. As David's plan failed, he resorted to a more sinister act. He ordered Uriah to be placed on the front line of a fierce battle, where he was ultimately killed. After Uriah's death, David took Bathsheba as his wife.

This story illustrates the moral failure and temptation that David faced. Despite being a man described as having a heart for God, David allowed his desires and impulses to lead him astray from God's commandments. The consequences of David's actions were severe, as he faced the loss of the child conceived through the affair and the repercussions of his deception and betrayal. Although David succumbed to temptation and committed grave sins, he later repented and sought forgiveness from God. The story serves as a reminder of the human frailty and the need for individuals to resist temptation and seek God's guidance and forgiveness when they fall into sin.

By examining David's experiences and the strategies

employed by his adversaries, we can uncover important lessons on how to overcome personal weaknesses and emerge stronger.

UNDERSTANDING PERSONAL WEAKNESSES

To effectively overcome personal weaknesses, it is crucial to recognize and understand them. David, known for his bravery and righteousness, fell victim to temptation when he encountered Bathsheba, the wife of Uriah. This episode serves as a reminder that no one is immune to personal weaknesses, regardless of their position or reputation. By acknowledging our vulnerabilities, we can take the first step towards addressing them. Matthew 26:41 encourages us to "Watch and pray so that you will not fall into temptation. The spirit is willing, but the flesh is weak." And in Psalm 51:10 ask God to "Create in me a pure heart, O God, and renew a steadfast spirit within me."

THE TEMPTATION

David's temptation illustrates the power of desire and the ability of external influences to exploit personal weaknesses. When David saw Bathsheba bathing, he allowed his desires to cloud his judgment and succumbed to the allure of the moment. This teaches us the importance of vigilance and self-control in the face of temptation, recognizing that succumbing to personal weaknesses can have severe consequences.

RECOGNIZING THE ENEMY'S DEVICES

The adversaries in David's story strategically exploited his weakness, showcasing the cunning devices of the enemy. David's adversary, in this case, was his own desire, which manipulated his judgment and led him astray. It is vital to identify the sources and triggers that can exacerbate personal weaknesses, as well as the tactics used by the enemy to exploit them.

DEVELOPING RESILIENCE

Overcoming personal weaknesses requires resilience and the ability to learn from mistakes. When confronted with his wrongdoing, David displayed remorse and sought forgiveness. Through this experience, he grew stronger and wiser, vowing to avoid succumbing to temptation in the future. It is crucial to develop resilience in the face of personal weaknesses, recognizing that setbacks can provide valuable lessons for personal growth.

SEEKING SUPPORT AND ACCOUNTABILITY

David's journey also emphasizes the significance of seeking support and accountability. After his transgression, David sought counsel from the prophet Nathan, who held him accountable for his actions. Establishing a support system and surrounding oneself with individuals who can provide guidance and hold one accountable can be instrumental in overcoming personal weaknesses.

The story of David serves as a cautionary tale, reminding us of the power of personal weaknesses and the temptations that can lead even the most virtuous astray. By understanding our vulnerabilities, recognizing the enemy's devices, developing resilience, and seeking support and accountability, we can navigate the challenges of personal weaknesses and emerge stronger. With a renewed sense of self-awareness and determination, we can overcome our weaknesses, achieve personal growth, and live a life of purpose and integrity.

When facing temptation, seeking God's help is a wise and powerful choice. The Bible offers guidance on how to turn to God for strength and deliverance. James 4:7-8 says "Submit yourselves, then, to God. Resist the devil, and he will flee from you. Come near to God and he will come near to you." The book of 1 Corinthians 10:13 states "No temptation has overtaken you except what is common to mankind. And God is faithful; he will not let you be tempted beyond what you can bear. But when you are tempted, he will also provide a way out so that you can endure it." James 1:5 also says, "If any of you lacks wisdom, you should ask God, who gives generously to all without finding fault, and it will be given to you."

Remember that when you face temptation, you can turn to God in prayer, study His Word, and rely on His promises. He is always ready to provide the strength and deliverance needed to overcome any temptation.

CHAPTER 4

Jezebel's Influence: Confronting Manipulative Spirits

In the realm of spiritual warfare, it is crucial for believers to be aware of the various strategies employed by the enemy. One such tactic is the influence of Jezebel, a manipulative spirit that seeks to undermine God's authority and hinder the advancement of His kingdom. By understanding and confronting this spirit, we can stand firm in our faith and protect ourselves from its deceptive tactics.

The story of Jezebel and her evil and manipulative influence can be found in the Old Testament, in the book of 1 Kings, chapter 16 to chapter 21. In 1 Kings 16:29-33, Jezebel introduced the worship of Baal and led the people of Israel into idolatry, causing them to turn away from the true God. In 1 Kings 21, her most notorious act is her involvement in the wrongful acquisition of Naboth's vineyard. Ahab desired Naboth's vineyard, but Naboth refused to sell it because it was an inheritance from his ancestors. Jezebel devised a plan to have Naboth falsely accused and executed, enabling Ahab to take possession of the vineyard. Jezebel promoted the worship of Baal and persecuted the prophets of the true God, Yahweh in 1 Kings 18. She encouraged Ahab to build altars for Baal and Asherah, leading to widespread idolatry in Israel.

These passages amongst others demonstrate Jezebel's influence in leading the people astray, promoting idolatry, persecuting God's prophets, and engaging in deceit and murder to accomplish her goals. Jezebel's actions serve as a cautionary tale in the Bible, illustrating the consequences of wickedness and manipulation.

RECOGNIZING JEZEBEL'S INFLUENCE

Jezebel, named after the notorious queen in the Bible, embodies the spirit of manipulation, control, and rebellion. This spirit operates through individuals who exhibit similar traits, both within and outside the church. It seeks to undermine God-given authority, sow discord, and manipulate others for personal gain. Identifying the signs of Jezebel's influence is the first step in confronting this spirit. Jacob's Deception of Isaac is an example of the spirit of manipulation where in Genesis 27, Jacob manipulates his father, Isaac, to receive the blessing intended for his brother, Esau. He dresses up as Esau and uses his father's blindness to deceive him. There's also the case of Delilah manipulating Samson's love for her to discover the secret of his strength, eventually leading to his downfall (Judges 16:15).

DECEPTIVE CHARISMA AND SEDUCTION

One of Jezebel's primary weapons is her ability to charm and deceive. Those under her influence often possess charismatic personalities that draw people in, making it difficult to discern their true intentions. They use seductive tactics to manipulate and control others, exploiting their weaknesses and vulnerabilities. Proverbs 7:6-27 warns against the seductive tactics of an immoral woman, cautioning against falling into her manipulative traps. Proverbs 26:24-26 says that "a malicious man disguises himself with his lips, but in his heart, he harbors deceit. Though his speech is charming, do not believe him, for seven abominations fill his heart." And in Matthew 18:6-7, "If anyone causes one of these little ones (those who believe in me) to stumble, it would be better for them to have a large millstone hung around their neck and to be drowned in the depths of the sea."

USURPING AUTHORITY

Jezebel desires to usurp and undermine godly authority structures. This spirit targets leaders, seeking to bring division, rebellion, and confusion within the church, families, workplaces, and other areas of influence. By sowing seeds of doubt, questioning legitimate authority, and fostering a spirit of rebellion, Jezebel aims to create chaos and hinder the work of God.

MANIPULATIVE TACTICS

Jezebel employs a range of manipulative tactics to maintain control over individuals and situations. These tactics include emotional manipulation, intimidation, flattery, and playing on people's insecurities. By exploiting their weaknesses, Jezebel seeks to gain power and manipulate others to fulfill their own agenda.

COUNTERACTING JEZEBEL'S INFLUENCE

Confronting Jezebel's influence requires a proactive and spiritual approach. Here are some key strategies to counteract this spirit:

- Discernment and Spiritual Wisdom: Developing discernment and seeking spiritual wisdom are essential in identifying and countering Jezebel's tactics. Through prayer, studying God's Word, and seeking counsel from mature believers, we can gain the discernment needed to recognize and confront manipulative spirits. A few bible passages that highlight the significance of discernment and spiritual wisdom include Proverbs 3:5-6, James 1:5, 1 Corinthians 2:14-15, and Colossians 1:9-10.

- Embracing Godly Authority: To counter Jezebel's influence, it is crucial to embrace and submit to God's ordained authority structures. This includes respecting and honoring leaders within the church, family, workplace, and society. Some Bible verses that speak about embracing and submitting to God's ordained authority structures include Romans 13:1-2, Hebrews 13:17, 1 Peter 2:13-15, Ephesians 5:21, and Colossians 3:22-23. By doing so, we align ourselves with God's design and create a strong defense against Jezebel's attacks.

- Cultivating a Spirit of Unity and Accountability: Jezebel thrives on division and isolation. By cultivating a spirit of unity and accountability within our relationships and communities, we create an environment that is resistant to Jezebel's manipulative tactics. This involves building healthy connections, fostering open communication, and standing together in love and truth. 1 Corinthians 12:25-27 says, "So that there should be no division in the body, but that its parts should have equal concern for each other. If one part suffers, every part suffers with it; if one part is honored, every part rejoices with it. Now you are the body of Christ, and each one of you is a part of it."

- Praying and Binding Jezebel's Influence: Engaging in fervent prayer and spiritual warfare is crucial in confronting Jezebel's influence. Through prayer, we can bind the power of this spirit and ask God to expose its tactics. Seeking the Holy Spirit's guidance and relying on His strength enables us to overcome Jezebel's manipulative influence. "For our struggle is not against flesh and blood, but against the rulers, against the authorities, against the powers of this dark world and against the spiritual forces of evil in the heavenly realms." - Ephesians 6:12 (NIV).

Confronting manipulative spirits such as Jezebel requires vigilance, discernment, and a reliance on God's wisdom and strength. By recognizing the devices of Jezebel and implementing effective countermeasures, we can protect ourselves, our communities, and our spiritual growth from its harmful influence. May we be equipped to stand firm in the face of manipulation and advance God's kingdom with discernment, unity, and love.

CHAPTER 5
Testing Job's Faith Amid Trials

In the biblical narrative of Job as found in the Book of Job in the Old Testament of the Bible, we find a remarkable story of faith, perseverance, and the testing of one's devotion to God. Job, a wealthy and righteous man, becomes the subject of a cosmic wager between God and Satan. Satan argues that Job's faith is merely a result of his prosperous life and challenges God to test him. Thus, Job's faith is put to the ultimate trial as he endures numerous afflictions and losses. Let's explore the devices used by the enemy in testing Job's faith and the lessons we can learn from his unwavering commitment to God.

LOSS OF MATERIAL POSSESSIONS

The enemy's first device in testing Job is to strip him of his wealth and possessions. In a swift succession of events, Job loses his livestock, servants, and even his children. The purpose behind this affliction is to strike at the core of Job's faith by removing the blessings he enjoyed and causing him to question God's goodness. Despite this immense loss, Job's response is remarkable: "Naked I came from my mother's womb, and naked I shall return there. The LORD gave and the LORD has taken away. Blessed be the name of the LORD." (Job 1:21)

Lesson: Job's example teaches us that our faith should not be based solely on material blessings. True faith endures even when our possessions are stripped away, for our ultimate trust lies in God and not in worldly treasures.

PHYSICAL AFFLICTIONS

Unsatisfied with Job's response to the loss of his possessions, the enemy proceeds to attack his health. Painful boils cover Job's body, bringing him to a state of suffering and misery. This physical affliction not only tests Job's physical endurance but also challenges his mental and emotional well-being. Job's wife, overwhelmed by the magnitude of their suffering, advises him to curse God and die. However, Job remains steadfast, refusing to give in to despair: "Shall we indeed accept good from God and not accept adversity?" (Job 2:10)

Lesson: Job's unwavering faith in the face of physical afflictions teaches us the importance of trusting God's sovereignty even in times of pain and suffering. Our faith is tested most profoundly when our bodies are weak, but it is during these times that we can experience God's comfort and strength.

WORDS OF ACCUSATION AND DOUBT

The enemy employs another device by sending Job's friends, who, rather than providing support, question his integrity and righteousness. Eliphaz, Bildad, and Zophar accuse Job of secret sins and imply that his suffering is a result of divine punishment. Their words add to Job's burden, pushing him to question God's justice and his own innocence. Nevertheless, Job clings to his faith, expressing his desire to present his case before God and affirming his trust in divine wisdom: "Though He slay me, yet will I hope in Him." (Job 13:15)

Lesson: Job's response to the accusations of his friends reminds us to remain steadfast in our faith, even when those around us doubt or accuse us unjustly. Our ultimate vindication comes from God alone, and His wisdom surpasses human understanding.

Job's story serves as a powerful testimony of faith amid trials. Through the devices of loss, physical afflictions, and words of accusation, the enemy sought to shake Job's trust in God. However, Job's unwavering commitment to his faith reveals the depth of his devotion and his profound understanding of God's sovereignty. As we face our own trials and tribulations, we can find inspiration in Job's example and draw strength from his enduring faith.

Here are a few Bible verses that speak about overcoming trials and hardships, drawing inspiration from the story of Job.

James 1:12: *"Blessed is the one who perseveres under trial because, having stood the test, that person will receive the crown of life that the Lord has promised to those who love him."*

Romans 5:3-4: *"Not only so, but we also glory in our sufferings, because we know that suffering produces perseverance; perseverance, character; and character, hope."*

1 Peter 5:10: *"And the God of all grace, who called you to his eternal glory in Christ, after you have suffered a little while, will himself restore you and make you strong, firm, and steadfast."*

Psalm 34:17-18: *"The righteous cry out, and the LORD hears them; he delivers them from all their troubles. The LORD is close to the brokenhearted and saves those who are crushed in spirit."*

Isaiah 41:10: *"So do not fear, for I am with you; do not be dismayed, for I am your God. I will strengthen you and help you; I will uphold you with my righteous right hand."*

2 Corinthians 4:17: "*For our light and momentary troubles are achieving for us an eternal glory that far outweighs them all.*"

Psalm 30:5: "*For his anger lasts only a moment, but his favor lasts a lifetime; weeping may stay for the night, but rejoicing comes in the morning.*"

1 Corinthians 10:13: "*No temptation has overtaken you except what is common to mankind. And God is faithful; he will not let you be tempted beyond what you can bear. But when you are tempted, he will also provide a way out so that you can endure it.*"

The story of Job teaches us the importance of remaining faithful and trusting in God even amid trials. These verses offer comfort, encouragement, and hope to those going through difficult times, reminding us that God is with us and will help us overcome.

CHAPTER 6

The Doubts Of Thomas: Building Stronger Belief Systems

In a world filled with diverse ideologies and conflicting belief systems, it is not uncommon for individuals to experience doubts and uncertainties about their own convictions. Just as Thomas, one of the disciples of Jesus, struggled with doubt, many people today face similar challenges in building and maintaining strong belief systems. This chapter explores the concept of doubt, its role in the formation of belief systems, and strategies for building stronger convictions.

UNDERSTANDING DOUBT

Doubt, at its core, is a natural human inclination to question and seek reassurance. It can arise from various sources such as intellectual inquiries, personal experiences, or external influences. Doubt challenges our existing beliefs and forces us to critically examine their validity. While doubt may initially cause unease, it also presents an opportunity for growth and a deeper understanding of our convictions.

THE DOUBTS OF THOMAS

The story of Thomas in the Gospel of John 20: 24-29, often referred to as "Doubting Thomas," provides an insightful example of doubt and its implications for belief systems. Thomas expressed skepticism when informed about Jesus' resurrection, demanding tangible evidence before accepting it as truth. However, when confronted with the evidence, his doubts transformed into unwavering faith. This narrative teaches us that doubts can be steppingstones towards stronger belief systems if addressed and resolved with an open mind.

EMBRACING DOUBT

Rather than viewing doubt as a weakness, it is crucial to embrace it as an essential part of personal growth. By acknowledging and exploring our doubts, we open ourselves to new perspectives and knowledge. Doubt becomes a catalyst for intellectual curiosity, encouraging us to engage in meaningful conversations, research, and introspection. It is through this process that our belief systems can evolve and become more resilient. The bible encourages us to "ask in faith, with no doubting, for the one who doubts is like a wave of the sea that is driven and tossed by the wind." - James 1:6.

STRATEGIES FOR BUILDING STRONGER BELIEF SYSTEMS

1. Honest Self-Reflection:

Engage in introspection to identify the underlying reasons for doubt. Examine your beliefs, values, and experiences that contribute to your current belief system. b. Seek Knowledge: Read and study diverse perspectives related to your beliefs. Explore opposing viewpoints to gain a comprehensive understanding of the subject matter. c. Dialogue and Debate: Engage in respectful discussions with others who hold different beliefs. This exchange of ideas challenges and strengthens our convictions. d. Personal Experience: Seek experiences that reinforce or challenge your beliefs. This can involve volunteering, traveling, or engaging in activities that expose you to different cultures and worldviews. e. Emotional Intelligence: Recognize and manage emotions that arise from doubt. Embrace uncertainty and be patient with yourself as you navigate through the process of building stronger beliefs.

2. The Role of Community:

Building strong belief systems is not solely an individual endeavor. The support and guidance of a community can play a vital role in shaping our convictions. Engage with like-minded individuals who share your beliefs, as well as those who respectfully challenge them. Participating in group discussions, attending religious or philosophical gatherings, or joining social communities centered around shared values can provide valuable insights and reinforce your belief system.

Doubt, far from being a hindrance, can serve as a catalyst for personal growth and the development of stronger belief systems. By embracing doubt and employing strategies such as self-reflection, seeking knowledge, engaging in dialogue, and nurturing a supportive community, individuals can cultivate resilient convictions. Just as Thomas's doubts were transformed into unwavering faith, so too can our doubts pave the way for a deeper and more meaningful understanding of our beliefs.

CHAPTER 7
The Pride Of Nebuchadnezzar: Humility And God's Sovereignty

In the book of Daniel in the Bible, we encounter the story of King Nebuchadnezzar, a powerful ruler who reigned over Babylon. Nebuchadnezzar was known for his strength, wealth, and military conquests, but he also possessed a flaw that would prove to be his downfall—pride.

Nebuchadnezzar's pride was evident in his actions and words. He boasted about his accomplishments, attributing them solely to his own power and might. He failed to acknowledge that his successes were ultimately a result of God's sovereignty and divine intervention.

God, in His infinite wisdom, decided to humble Nebuchadnezzar and teach him a valuable lesson about the dangers of pride. He sent a dream to the king, which Daniel, a prophet in Babylon, was able to interpret. The dream revealed that Nebuchadnezzar would be stripped of his power and glory, living like a wild animal in the fields until he acknowledged the authority of God.

Sure enough, Nebuchadnezzar's pride led to his downfall. As he walked on the roof of his palace, he arrogantly exclaimed, "Is not this great Babylon, which I have built by my mighty power as a royal residence and for the glory of my majesty?" (Daniel 4:30). Immediately, God's judgment fell upon him. He was driven away from human society and lived among the beasts of the field, eating grass like an ox, for a period of seven years (Daniel 5:20-21).

During this time, Nebuchadnezzar experienced a humbling transformation. His pride was replaced with humility as he recognized God's sovereignty. At the end of his appointed time, Nebuchadnezzar looked up to heaven, and his reason and understanding were restored. He praised and extolled the God of heaven, acknowledging His power and dominion over all.

Nebuchadnezzar's story serves as a powerful reminder of the dangers of pride and the importance of humility before God. It demonstrates that no matter how powerful or mighty we may perceive ourselves to be, we are ultimately subject to God's authority. Our accomplishments and successes are gifts from Him, and we should never forget to acknowledge His role in our lives.

Furthermore, the story emphasizes God's sovereignty over all things. He has the power to humble the proud and exalt the humble. Nebuchadnezzar's transformation illustrates that God's purpose will be accomplished, regardless of human pride or arrogance.

As we reflect on the story of Nebuchadnezzar, we are encouraged to cultivate a spirit of humility in our own lives (James 4:10: "Humble yourselves before the Lord, and he will lift you up."). We should recognize that our abilities and achievements are gifts from God and approach them with gratitude and humility. By acknowledging God's sovereignty and submitting ourselves to His will, we can avoid the pitfalls of pride and experience the blessings of a humble heart. "All of you, clothe yourselves with humility toward one another, because 'God opposes the proud but shows favor to the humble.' Humble yourselves, therefore, under God's mighty hand, that he may lift you up in due time." 1 Peter 5:5-6.

CHAPTER 8
The Betrayal Of Judas: Recognizing The Dangers Of Betrayal

Betrayal is a deeply painful and destructive act that has plagued humanity since time immemorial. It tears apart relationships, shatters trust, and inflicts emotional wounds that may never fully heal. One of the most infamous betrayals in history is that of Judas Iscariot, who famously betrayed Jesus Christ, leading to his crucifixion. Matthew 26:14-16 states, "Then one of the twelve, whose name was Judas Iscariot, went to the chief priests and said, 'What will you give me if I deliver him over to you?' And they paid him thirty pieces of silver. And from that moment he sought an opportunity to betray him." By examining the story of Judas, we can gain valuable insights into the dangers and consequences of betrayal.

THE BETRAYER'S MOTIVES

Betrayal often stems from a complex web of motives, ranging from personal gain to resentment, jealousy, or misguided beliefs. Judas, driven by greed and disillusionment, accepted thirty pieces of silver to betray Jesus. Understanding the underlying motives of a betrayer can shed light on their actions and help us recognize the warning signs.

DECEPTION AND MANIPULATION

The enemy employs deceit and manipulation to lull the betrayer into a false sense of security. Judas was influenced by Satan, who entered him and exploited his weaknesses. This highlights the subtle ways in which the enemy can twist a person's thoughts and emotions, leading them astray.

BREAKING TRUST

Betrayal shatters the foundation of trust that holds relationships together. Judas, who was trusted as one of Jesus' closest disciples, violated that trust by revealing Jesus' whereabouts to his enemies. The breach of trust can cause immense emotional pain, creating lasting scars that impact not only the betrayed but also the betrayer.

CONSEQUENCES OF BETRAYAL

Betrayal has far-reaching consequences, affecting not only individuals but also entire communities. In the case of Judas, his betrayal led to the arrest and crucifixion of Jesus, altering the course of history. Betrayal can unleash a cascade of negative outcomes, including broken relationships, damaged reputations, and even violence or loss of life.

THE POWER OF FORGIVENESS

While the act of betrayal is deeply painful, forgiveness has the power to heal and restore. Jesus, even in the face of betrayal, demonstrated extraordinary forgiveness, emphasizing the importance of extending grace and compassion to those who have wronged us. Forgiveness allows individuals and communities to break free from the cycle of betrayal and find the path to reconciliation.

GUARDING AGAINST BETRAYAL

Recognizing the dangers of betrayal equips us to guard against it in our own lives. Building strong relationships based on trust, open communication, and empathy can help minimize the likelihood of betrayal. Vigilance, discernment, and maintaining a healthy skepticism can also serve as protective measures against potential betrayers. To guard against betrayal, "But I say to you who hear, Love your enemies, do good to those who hate you, bless those who curse you, pray for those who abuse you (Luke 6:27-

28)." "Repay no one evil for evil but give thought to do what is honorable in the sight of all. If possible, so far as it depends on you, live peaceably with all. Beloved, never avenge yourselves, but leave it to the wrath of God, for it is written, 'Vengeance is mine, I will repay, says the Lord.' To the contrary, 'if your enemy is hungry, feed him; if he is thirsty, give him something to drink; for by so doing, you will heap burning coals on his head.' Do not be overcome by evil but overcome evil with good (Romans 12:17-21)."

The story of Judas serves as a cautionary tale, revealing the devastating consequences of betrayal. By understanding the devices employed by the enemy and recognizing the dangers of betrayal, we can actively work towards fostering trust, empathy, and forgiveness in our relationships. Through these efforts, we can strive to create a world where betrayal loses its power, and love and integrity prevail.

CHAPTER 9
The Fear Of Elijah: Overcoming Fear And Anxiety

In the journey of life, fear and anxiety often lurk in the shadows, seeking to hinder our progress and rob us of peace. Just as the biblical prophet Elijah faced his own fears and anxieties, we too must confront and overcome the challenges that arise in our lives. Elijah's story begins in 1 Kings 19 with a vivid description of the overwhelming fear that plagued him for years. He recounts sleepless nights, racing thoughts, and a constant sense of impending doom. He then experiences a divine encounter with God, where he expresses his feelings of despair and exhaustion, and God provides Elijah with reassurance, guidance, and a renewed sense of purpose.

UNDERSTANDING THE DEVICES OF FEAR AND ANXIETY

Fear and anxiety are complex emotions that can manifest in various forms, including worry, panic, and unease. They often stem from a sense of uncertainty, perceived threats, or traumatic experiences. By unraveling the devices fear and anxiety employ, we can better equip ourselves to combat them.

- **Distortion of Reality:** Fear and anxiety have a way of distorting our perception of reality, making situations appear worse than they are. Elijah, when faced with the threat of Queen Jezebel, believed he was the only faithful prophet left. There were many others who still stood for truth. Recognizing this distortion is crucial in overcoming fear.

- **Isolation and Loneliness:** Fear and anxiety thrive in isolation. They whisper lies that make us feel alone, abandoned, and vulnerable. Elijah experienced this when he fled to the wilderness, thinking he was the sole survivor. However, God reminded him that he was not alone and that there were others who shared his beliefs. Connecting with a supportive community can help alleviate feelings of isolation.

- **Overthinking and What-Ifs:** Fear and anxiety often trap us in a cycle of overthinking and dwelling on worst-case scenarios. Elijah, while hiding in the cave, fell into this pattern, questioning his purpose and contemplating death. Learning to manage overthinking by challenging irrational thoughts and focusing on the present moment can break the grip of fear.

OVERCOMING FEAR AND ANXIETY

Elijah's journey provides valuable insights and strategies to overcome fear and anxiety. By applying these principles, we can regain control of our lives and find peace amidst the storm.

- Seek Support: Just as Elijah received support from an angel and God's reassurance, we too should seek support from loved ones, mentors, or therapists. Opening about our fears and anxieties can bring comfort, guidance, and perspective. We can also seek support from the Bible to overcome fear and anxiety by finding comfort, guidance, and reassurance from its teachings. Some verses and principles that one can reflect on include Isaiah 41:10, Psalm 23:4, 1 Peter 5:7, Philippians 4:6-7, Romans 12:2, 1 John 4:18, 1 Thessalonians 5:16-18, Philippians 4:13, 2 Timothy 1:7, Psalm 46:10, and Joshua 1:9 which says, "Have

I not commanded you? Be strong and courageous. Do not be afraid; do not be discouraged, for the Lord your God will be with you wherever you go."

- Practice Self-Care: Taking care of our physical, emotional, and spiritual well-being is crucial in combating fear and anxiety. Elijah's encounter with God in the wilderness demonstrates the importance of self-care and seeking moments of rest, reflection, and rejuvenation. The bible teaches us in various books how to practice self-care and some of them include prayer and casting your cares in Philippians 4:6-7, finding rest in God in Matthew 11:28-30, practicing gratitude in 1 Thessalonians 5:18, taking care of your body in 1 Corinthians 6:19-20, focusing on positive and uplifting thoughts in Philippians 4:8, and letting go and surrendering in the book of Psalm 23:4. It is imperative to remember that self-care involves cultivating a deep and trusting relationship with God, aligning your thoughts and actions with his teachings, and seeking his guidance and comfort in times of fear and anxiety. Regularly engaging with these practices can help you find peace, strength, and resilience.

- Challenge Distorted Thinking: Identify and challenge the distorted thoughts that fuel fear and anxiety. Replace negative self-talk with positive affirmations and realistic perspectives. Elijah's encounter with

God's still, small voice teaches us to listen for truth amidst the noise of fear. Challenging distorted thinking from the bible to overcome fear and anxiety also involves adopting rational and balanced interpretations of biblical teachings. Philippians 4:6-7 encourages us, "do not be anxious about anything, but in every situation, by prayer and petition, with thanksgiving, present your requests to God. And the peace of God, which transcends all understanding, will guard your hearts and your minds in Christ Jesus." The book of Isaiah 41:10 also states, "so do not fear, for I am with you; do not be dismayed, for I am your God. I will strengthen you and help you; I will uphold you with my righteous right hand." Remember that challenging distorted thinking is an ongoing process that requires patience and self-compassion, and biblical wisdom can empower you to overcome fear and anxiety and experience a greater sense of peace and trust.

- Embrace Faith and Trust: Elijah's faith in God played a central role in his victory over fear. Cultivating faith and trust in God, as well as in ourselves, can provide the strength and courage needed to confront fear head-on. Some other steps one can take include prayer and meditation, scripture study (Psalm 34:4, Isaiah 41:10, Matthew 6:25-34, and Philippians 4:6-7), trusting in God's plan (Jeremiah 29:11, Romans 8:28), practicing gratitude, community and fellowship

(Hebrews 10:24-25), replacing negative thoughts, focusing on the present moment, practicing self-care, surrendering your fears and anxieties to God (Proverbs 3:5-6), and serving others by engaging in acts of kindness and service can take your focus off your own worries and help you experience the joy of making a positive impact on others' lives.

Fear and anxiety are formidable opponents that can hinder our personal growth and well-being. By understanding the devices employed by fear and drawing inspiration from Elijah's journey, we can develop strategies to overcome these emotional adversaries. Through seeking support, practicing self-care, challenging distorted thinking, and embracing faith and trust, we can unveil the devices of the enemy and triumph over fear and anxiety. Remember, just as Elijah emerged victorious, we too have the power to conquer our fears and live a life of courage, peace, and fulfillment.

CHAPTER 10

The Pharisees' Hypocrisy: Living With Authenticity

In the realm of spiritual warfare, it is crucial to identify and understand the tactics employed by the enemy. One striking example is the hypocrisy displayed by the Pharisees, a religious sect during the time of Jesus Christ. The Pharisees' hypocrisy from biblical times continues to resonate in today's world, as we often witness similar behaviors and attitudes among individuals and groups.

The Pharisees were a prominent religious group in the first century AD, known for their strict adherence to religious laws and traditions. They presented themselves as righteous and holy individuals, yet Jesus often exposed their hypocrisy. Their actions were characterized by a stark contrast between their outward appearances and inward intentions which can be found today in religious hypocrisy, double standards, judgmental attitudes, materialism and consumerism, political hypocrisy, selective morality, and authenticity and sincerity among others.

OUTWARD PIETY, INWARD CORRUPTION

The Pharisees meticulously followed the ceremonial laws and rituals, praying publicly, and giving alms to be seen by others. However, Jesus criticized them, stating that their motives were driven by a desire for public acclaim rather than genuine devotion to God (Matthew 6:5-6, Matthew 23:5-7). Their focus on external observance overshadowed the importance of cultivating a sincere and humble heart. In the realm of appearances, an ostentatious display of devotion prevails. A tapestry of outward piety meticulously woven, threads of righteousness carefully threaded through the fabric of public perception. Eyes are drawn to the grand gestures, the reverent words, and the ornate rituals meticulously performed. Yet, beneath this veneer of devoutness lies a concealed truth, a contradiction that festers in the shadows. In the sanctum of the heart, a different narrative unfolds. Like a chameleon, the soul adapts to the shades of duplicity, revealing an unsettling underbelly of inward corruption.

The fervent proclamations of faith cascade like waterfalls, yet the reservoirs of integrity run shallow. Benevolence paraded in broad daylight conceals selfish motives that scuttle like vermin in the night. The heart, meant to be a sanctuary, becomes a battleground for desires that erode the very foundation of sincerity. As one raises their voice in hymns of devotion, the echo of deception resonates through the hallowed halls of conscience. Embraces are warm, handshakes firm, but intentions are cold and slippery as ice. The tendrils of duplicity weave an intricate dance, ensnaring even the most ardent aspirations in their treacherous web.

The dichotomy between the exterior and the interior, the visible and the concealed, forms a haunting paradox. Like a fractured mirror, it reflects the dissonance between practiced righteousness and the tangled vines of moral decay. The conflict between the two creates a disconcerting dissonance that permeates the air. Yet, amid this disheartening portrayal, a glimmer of hope emerges. Recognizing the dissonance is the first step toward alignment. Awareness acts as a lantern, guiding the pilgrim's journey towards genuine redemption. The path to rectitude demands the courage to tear down the facade and confront the demons that lurk within.

Outward piety need not remain a mere facade; it can become a bridge to inner purity. By acknowledging the inconsistencies and confronting the veiled motives, the soul can embark on a transformative voyage. Through self-reflection, sincere repentance, and the cultivation of true virtue, the incongruity can be mended. In the end, the true measure of piety lies not in the splendor of the spectacle, but in the authenticity of the heart. The battle between outward appearances and inward integrity wages on, yet the potential for reconciliation remains ever-present. Through this struggle, the human spirit finds its strength, reshaping hypocrisy into a journey of growth and redemption.

As believers, it is vital to examine our own motivations behind religious practices (2 Corinthians 13:5). Are we seeking to please God and grow in our relationship with Him, or are we primarily concerned with impressing others? Authenticity before God should take precedence over the opinions of men.

JUDGMENTAL ATTITUDE

The Pharisees were quick to condemn others for their perceived shortcomings while failing to recognize their own faults. They imposed heavy burdens of legalism on people, focusing on trivial matters of the law rather than the weightier principles of justice, mercy, and faithfulness (Matthew 23:23-24). Jesus rebuked their hypocritical judgment, urging them to prioritize love and compassion.

As Christians, we must guard against adopting a judgmental attitude towards others. Instead, we should practice empathy and extend grace, recognizing our own flaws and the need for personal growth. Authenticity involves acknowledging our imperfections while embracing a spirit of love and acceptance.

In Matthew 7:1-2, we are told, "Do not judge, or you too will be judged. For in the same way, you judge others, you will be judged, and with the measure you use, it will be measured to you." And in Luke 6:37: "Do not judge, and you will not be judged. Do not condemn, and you will not be condemned. Forgive, and you will be forgiven." James 4:11-12 also states, "brothers and sisters, do not slander one another. Anyone who speaks against a brother or sister or judges them speaks against the law and judges it. When you judge the law, you are not keeping it, but sitting in judgment on it. There is only one Lawgiver and Judge, the one who can save and destroy. But you—who are you to judge your neighbor?"

The above verses emphasize the importance of not being quick to judge or condemn others, as we ourselves will be subject to judgment. Instead, the Bible encourages believers to treat others with kindness, forgiveness, and understanding, acknowledging that only God is the ultimate judge.

EXTERNAL RIGHTEOUSNESS, INTERNAL NEGLECT

The Pharisees meticulously observed external rituals, such as tithing and ceremonial cleansing, yet neglected the more significant aspects of the law—justice, mercy, and faithfulness (Matthew 23:23). Jesus emphasized the importance of genuine transformation of the heart, emphasizing that true righteousness flows from a sincere love for God and others.

In a world where appearances often reign supreme, the concept of external righteousness can easily take center stage. People strive to portray an image of moral uprightness, adhering to societal norms and values that define what is deemed 'right' and 'just'. This external display of virtue can range from public acts of kindness to vocal expressions of support for noble causes. It's the kind of righteousness that garners praise, admiration, and acceptance from those around us. However, amidst this fervor for maintaining a faultless image on the surface, there exists a perilous pitfall - the neglect of one's internal landscape. This internal neglect refers to the disregard or oversight of personal emotional, psychological, and ethical well-being. It's the tendency to prioritize the façade over genuine self-improvement and reflection.

Consider a person who vehemently advocates for humanitarian causes in public forums, yet privately harbors resentment and animosity towards their own family members. Or picture a company that touts its commitment to employee welfare and work-life balance yet fosters a toxic work environment behind closed doors. These scenarios illustrate the stark dissonance between what is projected outwardly and the hidden truths that lie within. Internal neglect can manifest in various ways, such as suppressing emotions, avoiding introspection, or failing to address one's own flaws and biases. It's akin to meticulously maintaining the exterior of a house while allowing its foundation to crumble. In the long run, this neglect can lead to inner turmoil, strained relationships, and a fractured sense of self.

Authenticity demands a holistic approach to spirituality. We should not neglect the internal transformation of our hearts while focusing solely on outward actions. A genuine relationship with God should produce a heart that is compassionate, just, and faithful. The pursuit of external righteousness should never come at the cost of internal neglect. Striving to be morally upright and virtuous is commendable, but it must be accompanied by a parallel effort to cultivate one's own emotional, psychological, and ethical well-being. Balancing both aspects allow for a more authentic, harmonious, and impactful existence, where the outer facade aligns harmoniously with the inner truth.

The example of the Pharisees serves as a powerful reminder of the dangers of hypocrisy and the need for authenticity in our spiritual journeys. Living with authenticity involves aligning our inward motivations with our outward actions, cultivating a non-judgmental attitude, and pursuing a genuine transformation of the heart. By learning from the mistakes of the Pharisees, we can strive to live with authenticity, glorifying God in all aspects of our lives.

CHAPTER 11

Peter's Denial: Embracing Forgiveness And Restoration

In the biblical narrative, Peter's denial of Jesus stands out as a poignant moment filled with lessons on forgiveness and restoration. This event serves as a powerful example of human weakness, the consequences of denying one's faith, and the transformative power of forgiveness. Let us delve into the story of Peter's denial found in all four Gospels of the New Testament: Matthew

26:69-75, Mark 14:66-72, Luke 22:54-62, and John 18:15-18, 25-27, exploring the insights it offers and the lessons we can apply to our own lives.

The Depths of Human Weakness: Peter, known for his loyalty and passion, found himself facing a test of faith when Jesus was arrested. Despite his previous claims of unwavering dedication, Peter succumbed to fear and denied knowing Jesus not just once, but three times. This moment exposes the fragility of human nature and serves as a reminder that even the most devoted individuals can falter under challenging circumstances. Throughout the Bible, there are other instances where human weakness and tests of faith are prominent themes. These stories often showcase the struggles, doubts, and vulnerabilities of individuals, highlighting their journeys of faith and personal growth. Some of those instances include that of Abraham and Isaac, Job, Moses and the Israelites, Doubting Thomas, and Garden of Gethsemane.

CONSEQUENCES OF DENIAL

Peter's denial of Jesus had immediate consequences, both internally and externally. Internally, he experienced profound guilt and shame for his actions. Externally, his denial positioned him among those who opposed Jesus, distancing him from the fellowship and teachings he cherished. This highlights the repercussions of denying one's faith and the potential damage it can cause to personal relationships and spiritual growth.

JESUS' UNFATHOMABLE FORGIVENESS

Despite Peter's denial, Jesus demonstrated unparalleled forgiveness and understanding. After His resurrection, Jesus appeared to Peter and offered him an opportunity for redemption. By questioning Peter three times, "Do you love me?" Jesus allowed him to express his commitment, thereby giving Peter a chance to reaffirm his devotion and restore their relationship. Jesus' forgiveness shows us that no matter how far we may have strayed, there is always a path to reconciliation and renewal. Jesus' forgiveness provides us with spiritual healing, emotional relief, personal growth, restored relationships, and strengthened faith.

RESTORATION AND COMMISSIONING

In embracing forgiveness, Peter experienced a profound transformation. The restoration of their relationship empowered Peter to fulfill his purpose as a leader in the early Christian community. On the day of Pentecost, filled with the Holy Spirit, Peter boldly proclaimed the message of Jesus to a multitude, leading to the conversion of thousands. This demonstrates the transformative power of forgiveness and the potential for growth and effectiveness in serving others.

Peter's denial and subsequent restoration offer valuable lessons for us today. They teach us that no one is immune to moments of weakness and that even our most significant failures can be redeemed. The story invites us to examine our own lives, acknowledge our shortcomings, and seek forgiveness. It reminds us of the importance of extending forgiveness to others, just as Jesus forgave Peter. Additionally, it encourages us to embrace restoration and use our past experiences to grow and positively impact the lives of those around us.

Peter's denial and subsequent restoration present a profound narrative of human weakness, forgiveness, and restoration. Through this account, we gain insights into our own vulnerabilities, the consequences of denying our faith, and the transformative power of forgiveness. As we reflect on Peter's journey, let us strive to embrace forgiveness and restoration, both in our relationship with God and with others, knowing that through these acts, we can experience profound personal growth and contribute to the betterment of society.

CHAPTER 12

The Rebellion Of Korah: Submission To God-Ordained Authority

The rebellion of Korah, as described in Numbers 16:1–40, serves as a powerful example of the consequences of challenging or rebelling against God-ordained authority. This story can provide insights into the importance of submission to authority and the dangers of pride and rebellion.

In the Book of Numbers, Korah, along with Dathan, Abiram, and 250 other prominent Israelites, revolted against

Moses and Aaron, who were appointed by God as leaders of the Israelites. Korah and his followers questioned the authority and leadership of Moses and Aaron, expressing their dissatisfaction with the way they were being governed. They accused Moses and Aaron of exalting themselves above the congregation and sought to seize their positions of leadership. In a contemporary context, the "rebellion of Korah" could be used to describe situations where there is dissent or disagreement within the church community, particularly regarding leadership, authority, or theological beliefs. This could involve members of a church questioning the decisions or teachings of their leaders, or even a split within the congregation over differing interpretations of doctrine.

The Rebellion of Korah did not go unnoticed by God. He intervened and instructed Moses to gather the rebels and conduct a test to determine whom He had chosen as His representatives. The next day, Moses instructed Korah and his followers to bring censers with incense before the Lord. Moses and Aaron did the same. Then, the glory of the Lord appeared before the entire congregation, and God spoke, affirming His choice of Moses and Aaron as His appointed leaders.

Because of their rebellion, the ground beneath Korah and his followers split open, swallowing them and everything they possessed. This served as a clear demonstration of God's judgment against those who rebelled against His chosen authority. The rebellion of Korah resulted in severe punishment and loss of life, showing the seriousness of challenging God-ordained leadership.

This biblical account teaches several important lessons. First, it highlights the significance of submission to authority. God has established authority structures in various realms of life, including government, family, and spiritual leadership. Submission to these authorities is essential for maintaining order and harmony. Challenging or rebelling against God-ordained authority can lead to dire consequences, both in the spiritual and natural realms.

Second, the story of Korah warns against pride and self-exaltation. Korah and his followers sought to elevate themselves and their own desires above God's chosen leaders. They disregarded the authority that God had established and acted out of their own selfish ambitions. This serves as a reminder to approach positions of authority with humility and a willingness to serve, rather than seeking personal gain or glory.

Lastly, the account of Korah's rebellion emphasizes the importance of discernment and wisdom. It is crucial to carefully discern God's appointed authorities and submit to them accordingly. This requires seeking God's guidance and relying on His Word to recognize and honor the leaders He has established. Romans 13:1-7 emphasizes the importance of submitting to governing authorities, as they are established by God. Jesus also addressed the issue of taxes and governmental authority in Mark 12:13-17, emphasizing rendering to Caesar what belongs to Caesar. In Hebrews 13:17, God instructs believers to obey and submit to their spiritual leaders, as these leaders watch over their souls and will give an account. Ultimately, the Bible emphasizes submitting to God as the highest authority. In James 4:7, believers are told to submit to God and resist the devil.

The rebellion of Korah in the Bible serves as a cautionary tale about the dangers of challenging or rebelling against God-ordained authority. It underscores the significance of submission, humility, and discernment in our relationship with authority. By learning from this biblical example, we can strive to honor and respect the authority structures God has put in place while avoiding the pitfalls of rebellion and pride.

CHAPTER 13

The Manipulation Of Delilah: Guarding Against Emotional Manipulation

Emotional manipulation is a powerful tactic that the enemy often employs to deceive and manipulate individuals. Throughout history, we find numerous examples, even in the Bible, where individuals fell victim to emotional manipulation, leading to dire consequences. One such example is the story of Delilah and Samson.

In the book of Judges 16:4-22, we encounter the story of Samson, a man of great physical strength, and Delilah, a woman who conspired against him. Delilah was approached by the Philistine lords who sought to capture and subdue Samson. Sensing an opportunity to exploit Samson's weakness, Delilah agreed to help them.

THE PROCESS OF EMOTIONAL MANIPULATION

Emotional manipulation is a tactic used by individuals to control or influence the emotions, thoughts, and behaviors of others for their own benefit. It often involves subtle or covert techniques aimed at exploiting someone's vulnerabilities or insecurities. Delilah initiated a relationship with Samson, gradually gaining his trust and affection. Emotional manipulators often seek to build strong emotional connections before exploiting their victims.

Delilah observed Samson's source of strength and understood that it lay in his hair, which had never been cut. Manipulators keenly identify their targets' vulnerabilities to exploit them later. Delilah also used her intimacy with Samson to repeatedly question him about the secret of his strength. She feigned emotional distress and longing, using her words and actions to appeal to Samson's love for her. Emotional manipulators skillfully play on their victims' emotions to gain control.

Delilah's repeated attempts to extract the secret from Samson demonstrated the manipulative technique of gradual escalation. Each time, she claimed that Samson did not truly love her unless he shared his secret, thereby pressuring him further. The technique of gradual escalation is a common tactic used by manipulators to achieve their goals by wearing down resistance and increasing the target's vulnerability through a series of incremental steps. It preys on emotions, trust, and psychological pressure to achieve compliance or disclosure of information.

THE CONSEQUENCES OF EMOTIONAL MANIPULATION

Samson's love for Delilah clouded his judgment, rendering him vulnerable to manipulation. Like Delilah, emotional manipulators exploit their victims' emotions to weaken their resolve and influence their decisions. Ultimately, Samson succumbed to Delilah's relentless emotional manipulation and revealed the secret of his strength. As a result, his hair was cut, and he lost his supernatural power. The enemy often seeks to strip us of our spiritual strength and hold us captive through emotional manipulation.

It's important to recognize the signs of emotional manipulation and seek support if you believe you are being manipulated or if you suspect someone you know is engaging in manipulative behavior. Establishing boundaries, seeking therapy, and building a strong support network can be crucial steps toward healing and recovering from the consequences of emotional manipulation.

GUARDING AGAINST EMOTIONAL MANIPULATION

It is important for every Christian to recognize the signs of emotional manipulation, such as excessive guilt-tripping, constant criticism, or intense emotional demands. Develop discernment to identify when someone is trying to exploit your emotions. Christians must also surround themselves with wise and trustworthy individuals who can provide guidance and offer a different perspective. They can help you recognize emotional manipulation and provide support during challenging situations. Establish clear boundaries in relationships to protect oneself from emotional manipulation. Be firm in maintaining those boundaries and communicate your needs and expectations clearly. Build a strong foundation of truth through prayer, studying the Word of God, and seeking a personal relationship with Him. The enemy's tactics are often based on deception, but the truth of God's Word can help guard your heart and mind.

The Bible offers valuable insights and principles that can help guard against emotional manipulation. Proverbs 2:10-11 - "For wisdom will enter your heart, and knowledge will be pleasant to your soul. Discretion will protect you, and understanding will guard you." Developing wisdom and discernment can help you recognize and resist emotional manipulation. Proverbs 3:5-6 - "Trust in the Lord with all your heart and lean not on your own understanding; in all your ways submit to him, and he will make your paths straight." Relying on God's guidance can help you navigate situations where emotional manipulation might be present. Proverbs 14:7 - "Stay away from a fool, for you will not find knowledge on their lips." Sometimes, the best defense against emotional manipulation is to distance yourself from manipulative individuals.

The story of Delilah and Samson serves as a powerful reminder of the dangers of emotional manipulation. By understanding the enemy's tactics and implementing measures to guard against them, we can protect ourselves from falling into the trap of manipulation. Through awareness, discernment, seeking wisdom, setting boundaries, and grounding ourselves in truth, we can overcome emotional manipulation and walk in the freedom and strength that God has given us.

CHAPTER 14

The Frustration Of Jonah: Surrendering To God's Will

In Jonah 4, we find the account of Jonah who was faced with trials, temptations, and frustrations while trying to fulfill God's will. Jonah was a prophet who initially resisted God's command, leading to frustration and eventual surrender.

Jonah was a prophet whom God commanded to go to the city of Nineveh and proclaim its impending destruction due to its wickedness. Instead of immediately obeying, Jonah chose to resist God's call. He boarded a ship headed in the opposite direction, attempting to flee from God's presence. Jonah's disobedience highlights the enemy's strategy of enticing us to ignore God's command and pursue our own desires.

As Jonah sailed away from God's intended path, a great storm arose, threatening to destroy the ship. This storm was a direct consequence of Jonah's disobedience and the enemy's attempt to hinder God's plan. The sailors, realizing that Jonah was the cause of their distress, confronted him. In our own lives, the enemy often employs external circumstances to challenge us when we resist God's will.

Jonah recognized his rebellion and acknowledged that his disobedience had caused trouble not only for himself but also for those around him. Realizing the futility of his actions, he surrendered to God's will and allowed himself to be thrown into the sea. God's response was immediate. He sent a great fish to swallow Jonah, providing him with a temporary refuge. In Jonah's surrender, we see the enemy's devices exposed, as the storm ceased, and Jonah found redemption.

Prayer and Restoration: From within the belly of the fish, Jonah cried out to God in repentance and submission. God, in His mercy, heard Jonah's prayer and caused the fish to vomit him onto dry land. This demonstrates the enemy's failure to keep us in captivity when we turn to God with a humble heart. Jonah's restoration serves as a reminder that surrendering to God's will brings about forgiveness, reconciliation, and renewed purpose.

The story of Jonah offers profound insights into the devices of the enemy and the importance of surrendering to God's will. By submitting oneself to God, a person becomes more aware of the tactics, schemes, or strategies used by the enemy. Through Jonah's journey, we learn that resistance to God's command can lead to frustration and turmoil. However, by recognizing our rebellion and choosing to surrender, we can experience restoration and fulfillment of God's plan for our lives. May we heed the lessons from Jonah's story, embracing God's will wholeheartedly and finding peace in surrendering to His divine guidance.

In James 4:7-8 we are asked to "submit yourselves, then, to God. Resist the devil, and he will flee from you. Come near to God and he will come near to you." "Be alert and have a sober mind. Your enemy the devil prowls around like a roaring lion looking for someone to devour. Resist him, standing firm in the faith, because you know that the family of believers throughout the world is undergoing the same kind of sufferings (1 Peter 5:8-9)."

CHAPTER 15

The Battles Of Paul: Perseverance And Endurance In Ministry

The apostle Paul was one whose life and ministry served as a profound source of inspiration for believers today. Let us delve into Paul's battles, by exploring the theme of perseverance and endurance in ministry. By examining the challenges, he encountered, the devices of the enemy he unveiled, and the insights we can glean, we will gain valuable lessons applicable to our own spiritual journeys.

The Conversion and Calling of Paul (Acts 9:1-19): The apostle Paul, formerly known as Saul, was a fervent persecutor of Christians. However, his life took a dramatic turn on the road to Damascus when he encountered the risen Christ. This divine encounter not only transformed Paul's heart but also marked the beginning of his ministry. From the outset, Paul faced opposition and resistance from both the religious authorities and those who were skeptical of his conversion. Yet, he persevered, relying on the calling and purpose God had entrusted to him.

PERSECUTION AND IMPRISONMENT

Paul's commitment to spreading the Gospel brought him face-to-face with persecution and imprisonment. He endured beatings, stoning, and various forms of physical and emotional suffering. Despite these adversities, Paul remained steadfast in his mission, considering it a privilege to suffer for the sake of Christ. Through his endurance, he demonstrated the power of God's grace and the resilience of a faith rooted in unwavering conviction.

SPIRITUAL WARFARE AND DECEPTION

(2 Cor. 2:11; 10:3–6; 11:14; 12:7): In Paul's letters, we gain insights into the spiritual battles he faced. He warned believers about the devices of the enemy, emphasizing the importance of staying vigilant and putting on the whole armor of God. Paul recognized the deceptive tactics employed by the adversary, such as false teachings, divisive

spirits, and the temptation to compromise the truth. His teachings remind us of the ongoing spiritual warfare we encounter in ministry and the need to rely on God's wisdom and discernment.

THORNS IN THE FLESH

Paul's battles extended beyond external persecution. He also wrestled with personal challenges, including a "thorn in the flesh." While the nature of this thorn remains unclear, it served as a constant reminder of his dependence on God's grace. Instead of removing the thorn, God assured Paul that His strength would be made perfect in weakness. This revelation taught Paul the value of humility, relying on God's power rather than his own abilities.

THE ULTIMATE VICTORY

Despite enduring numerous trials, Paul's perseverance and endurance led to significant achievements in his ministry. His writings, missionary journeys, and establishment of churches continue to impact generations of believers. Moreover, Paul's unwavering faith in the face of adversity serves as an encouragement for all believers striving to fulfill their God-given purposes. Ultimately, Paul's battles culminated in the eternal victory he anticipated, as he looked forward to receiving the crown of righteousness from the Lord.

The battles of Paul provide us with profound insights

into the theme of perseverance and endurance in ministry. His unwavering commitment to the Gospel, even in the face of intense opposition, serves as an inspiration for believers today. By understanding the devices of the enemy, remaining steadfast in faith, and relying on God's strength, we can navigate our own spiritual battles with courage and perseverance. Just as Paul triumphed, we too can experience the ultimate victory that comes from faithfully pursuing our calling in Christ.

CONCLUSION

The Bible provides us with numerous examples and insights into the devices and tactics used by the enemy, often referred to as Satan/devil. These examples serve as valuable lessons and warnings for believers, equipping them to recognize and overcome the enemy's schemes.

One of the key devices used by the enemy is deception. We see this illustrated in the Garden of Eden when Satan deceived Adam and Eve, leading them to doubt God's word and rebel against His command. This highlights the importance of knowing and holding fast to God's truth, for it is the ultimate weapon against deception.

Another device employed by the enemy is temptation, especially that of Jesus found in the Gospels of Matthew, Mark, and Luke. Jesus faced intense temptation in the wilderness, where Satan sought to entice Him with power, fame, and worldly possessions. Jesus' response serves as a model for believers, demonstrating the power of relying on the Word of God and resisting temptation through faith and obedience.

The enemy also seeks to sow discord and division among believers. In the New Testament, we find numerous instances where false teachers and divisive individuals infiltrated the early Christian communities, spreading heresies and causing strife. The apostles warned against such influences and encouraged believers to stand firm in unity and love, being discerning and rooted in the truth.

Moreover, the enemy often attacks believers through discouragement and doubt. In the story of Job, Satan sought to undermine Job's faith by inflicting immense suffering and loss. However, Job remained steadfast, holding on to his trust in God despite his circumstances. This teaches us the importance of persevering in faith, even in the face of trials and adversity.

Ultimately, the Bible assures us that the victory over the enemy has been won through Jesus Christ. In His death and resurrection, Jesus triumphed over sin, death, and all the devices of the enemy. As believers, we are called in Ephesians 6:11 to "put on the armor of God, so that we can take our stand against the devil's schemes", standing firm in His truth, righteousness, peace, faith, salvation, and the Word of God.

By studying the devices of the enemy as revealed in the Bible, we gain valuable insights and wisdom to navigate the spiritual battles we face. We are reminded to be vigilant, prayerful, and rooted in God's Word, for it is through Him that we can resist the enemy and experience the abundant life that God has promised us.

May we continually seek God's guidance, rely on His strength, and walk in the victory that is ours through Jesus Christ, knowing that He has overcome the devices of the enemy.

UNVEILING THE DEVICES OF THE ENEMY

www.ingramcontent.com/pod-product-compliance
Lightning Source LLC
LaVergne TN
LVHW020428080526
838202LV00055B/5081